The Comfort Coloring Book

Christina Brittain

Balboa Press books may be ordered through booksellers or by contacting:

Balboa Press
A Division of Hay House
1663 Liberty Drive
Bloomington, IN 47403
www.balboapress.com
1 (877) 407-4847

ISBN: 978-1-5043-4459-3 (sc)
ISBN: 978-1-5043-4458-6 (e)

Print information available on the last page.

Balboa Press rev. date: 11/25/2015

This book is dedicated to the fact of well-being.

Acknowledgments

It is a breathtaking thing to realize how MANY angels participated in the creation of this book! And to realize that the book itself called in the perfect and necessary midwives to usher it in!

To my dear circle of friends far and wide, and to my remarkable clients and students, you have loved and encouraged me in countless, beautiful ways. Each of you contributes more love, joy and support than you'll ever know!

To Sunny Sangster, the computer goddess with a heart of gold! You have a true and shining genius, and I'm deeply grateful you blessed this book with it!

To my assistant Erin Brown, your skills and attention are so nuanced, graceful and powerful! I appreciate you with all my heart!

To my soul cousin Katie Autote, thank you for the pics, the playfulness and the deep and enduring friendship. I love you Prima!

To Billie Ann Franchella, thank you for showing up in Maui for our Divine play date! I'm sure the fun we've been having – and have planned – has been in The Works for a while! Thank you for the countless expansive phone calls. And for getting goosebumps when I first told you about the coloring books. I love you so much!

To Lane, Nancy, Allison and Ruth who lent me their fabulous editing skills!

To the flat-out amazing Lane Blake! No words can express how much you have blessed me. I am in awe of your generosity and how MANY ways you have shared your light and talents with me. You were a major catalyst for this project and I am honored that you believed in my work long before the coloring books were even a twinkle in my eye. I love you!

To Nancy O'Fallon, we clearly showed up in each other's lives on schedule! Thank you for your authentic, powerful being and for sharing it with me. I'm so glad we get to journey together!

To Allison Rolfe, honey, you just "get" this book! Probably because the book had you in mind all along! I am moved beyond gratitude for the endless ways you poured love toward me during this entire project. You are an extraordinary being, and it gives me huge joy that you know that.

continued....

To my shaman-mystic-wise-woman friend Ruth Watson, the way you live is mastery. The way you be is a light house. Time and again on this journey it helps point me home to myself and my true frequency. Thank you for the many ways you are so present and loving. Thank you for being so You.

And huge thanks to whatever Loving Force dropped the inspiration for the coloring books into my head! I feel privileged to have been invited into such a radically uplifting project. It has changed me in its brilliant fire of transformation, and given me a sweet and powerful means to share love as only I can.

And to all of you reading this book, thank you from the depths of my soul for all that YOU contribute to Everything, and for effortlessly sharing love as only you all can.

Introduction

This book loves you. It adores you. It's so happy to tell you that. It's gazing up at you, moved by how completely special you are. It's beaming warmth, hugs and smiles at you right now. Every page in this book is celebrating you. Each drawing asked to be included so it could remind you how extraordinary you are. Without trying, just by being you, you make everything better. You matter. You contribute. You add more awesome to the universe. It's true. You don't have to do anything or try for it to be true. It just is. You are good. It's just who you are. It's built into your blueprint. And life loves you. You can relax, enjoy, and just be.

Kids really get this. If you've ever seen a small child playing with a dog, there's no difference between them: neither one of them is trying to do anything. They're just playing. They're just present. They're being what they are. Effortless. Joyful. Alive!

Coloring has the amazing ability to instantly transport us to that childlike way of being. There's a timeless quality and spaciousness that comes with coloring. It returns us to a natural state of ease, freedom and simplicity. We're reconnected with our innate and healthy human functions of play, dreaming, and utter and complete relaxation in the present moment.

Recently I was doing some shopping, and the saleswoman and I got to talking. The second I mentioned coloring books, her whole body visibly relaxed, her face got softer and brighter, and there seemed to be more space and breath all around her. "Oh, I love coloring books!" She gushed, smiling and turning towards me excitedly. I swear she looked younger! She immediately started telling me about a time when she was in college and got the flu. She'd gone to get some soup and some things from the drug store. She happened upon some coloring books and thought, "Ahh! I haven't colored in years. That's the perfect thing for me right now." She bought the coloring books and some crayons, went home with her soup, and spent some happy days convalescing, actually glad to have the excuse to color. "Ever since then," she told me, "I keep my own stash of crayons. I'm a mom now so I keep my crayons in a jar up high where my daughter can't get them. One day my daughter saw them and asked about them, and I told her those were mommy's special crayons so she'd have to use her own. We color together too, but I wait until after she goes to bed to use my crayons." The saleswoman had forgotten me for the moment, and I was moved by her deep and obvious love, both for her child, and for the crayons she kept for herself. "I've been thinking lately that I need to get some pens and colored pencils too," she trailed off dreamily.....

I LOVED hearing the woman's story. I love that she recognized early in her adult life that coloring is still available to her. I love that she gives herself time and space to do it regularly. I love that it obviously uplifts and rejuvenates her. But most of all, I love that she honors herself by having her own special crayons. For her, coloring is more than relaxing; it's an act of self love.

continued...

This book is all about that self love. Because it's a coloring book it can help you step into that easy childlike way of being. But while you are in that relaxed state, it also reminds you about how wonderful you are and how much you are loved. This is a comfort coloring book – a place to be soothed and loved back into knowing that all is well. The words and images are all saying, "Hi, honey. I love you. Life loves you. Don't forget how wonderful you are. Remember to be nice to you. Remember to listen to you and adore you. We do!"

Every page in this book wants you to know it recognizes your specialness. Each page is a love letter in amazement of how much you offer the world just by being yourself. This book truly loves you, and I am so happy it gets to tell you that.

All my love and amazement too,

Christina Brittain
September 2015

Feel free to.....

1. Color outside the lines (or not!).
2. Toss out any ideas about what color things are "supposed" to be.
3. Add your own words.
4. Use crayons, pens, colored pencils, pastels, paint, glitter, sequins, stickers, magazine cutouts, feathers....(you get the idea).
5. Draw in extra stuff – a mustache on that flower? Polka dots on that bear?
6. Write journal entries on the back (or front) of the drawings.
7. Color only part of a picture.
8. Skip through the book or go sequentially.
9. Color on your lunch break to relax and reset.
10. Color with friends over a glass of wine – or coffee and cake!
11. Color in silence – or with your favorite music – whatever feels best.
12. Color under your bedspread with a flashlight.
13. Color alone for quiet time or meditation.
14. Color with your kids, your parents, your siblings or your spouse.
15. Make photocopies of pictures of yourself and loved ones, then glue your faces on the figures and objects on the drawings!
16. Mail one to a friend – color it in, or send it blank with some crayons in the envelope.
17. Hang your favorite drawings on the wall of your office, bedroom or kitchen.
18. Take apart the book and hang all the drawings together on a wall. Your own personal oracle.
19. Color in the book together with your family or a dear group of friends. You'll create a special book you can all cherish. Or take each of your colored pages out of the book and hang them up together as a community "quilt."
20. Sing songs while you color.
21. Dance while you color.
22. Do yoga while you color.
23. Light a candle or incense while you color.
24. Read the words out loud to yourself.
25. Enjoy the simplicity of the line drawings and don't color at all.
26. Give yourself every freedom possible – with this book and in life in general!

And now a deep breath…

Proceed
from
within...

Proceed from within

Honestly
the only opinion that really matters
is yours.
Do what is right for you
and you'll end up living –
fully living! –
your own true life!
Give yourself that freedom!
That right!
That joy of discovery!

Be who you are
and love it!

Be who you are

You are a completely unique creature
with your own care and feeding
and your own ways of being –
that are awesome!
No one could be you even if they tried!
And if you tried to be somebody else
the world would be denied
the particular
special
wonderfulness of You!
Be You on purpose
with wholehearted celebration –
just like you intended all along!

Everything is Divine
It just makes sense
to love myself
Including Me.

Everything is Divine

It's not that there's the Universe out there
and then, well, there's you.
You ARE the Universe.
One.
The same.
Inseparable.
Love you
and you bestow love
on all Creation.

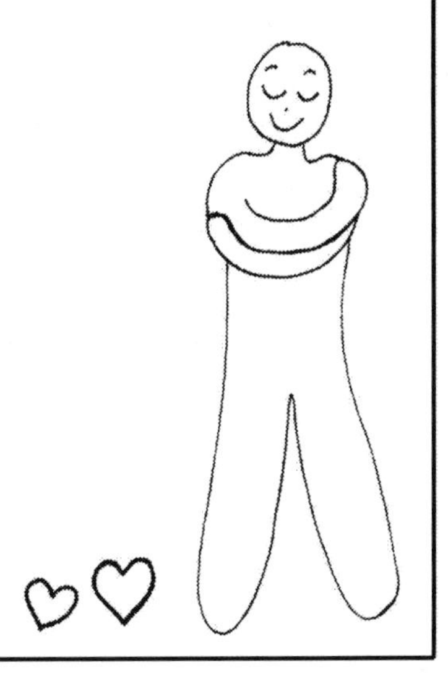

Perfect!!
Please turn book this way!

<u>Cosmic hug</u>

Every once in a while
remember to feel for it –
the Universe is hugging you all the time.
You are seen.
You are held.
You are powerfully loved.

We
all
belong

We all belong

Infinity includes everything
and everyone.
There is endless diversity
for limitless options, expansion and joy!
Every difference is exquisitely valuable!
There are no spare parts
and each part
makes The Big Picture
infinitely more beautiful.
YOU
make Infinity
more beautiful.

Excuse me, are you my angel?
YES!
Yes!
Yes!
Yes!
Yes!
Yes!
Yes
Yes
Yes!
YES!

All the angels

What if all the angels
are YOUR angels?
What if you're supported
by seen and unseen forces
all the time?
What if you're just THAT important?
(You are!)

I am worthy

Worthy

Worthy is just a word
that humans made up.
The Universe just laughs at that silliness
and waits for you
to remember your own magnificence!
Your infinite goodness!
Your oneness
with Divinity Itself!

I let myself receive!
of course
yin-yang, baby!
YES!! THANK YOU!!
It's a natural flow!!

Receive!

Giving and receiving
are two ways that the magic of Love
moves through us.
Don't be lopsided!
Don't throw a monkey wrench in the flow of all good things.
Let receiving be as natural as giving.
Accept help from others.
Celebrate gifts!
Embrace praise.
Allow the easy paths and circumstances.
Open your heart to the perfect ebb and flow –
the in breath and out breath –
of the abundant Universe Itself.

I take
time to
listen
in

Take time to listen

You really can slow down
for whatever wants to be shared.
Simply being with the peaceful presence of Yourself
is realigning.
And sometimes there is more that wants to be said
from the vast knowing inside you.
Guidance.
Insight.
Clarity.
Maybe even a joke or two!
It's all right there
in the relationship with You!
You
are so worthy of listening to.

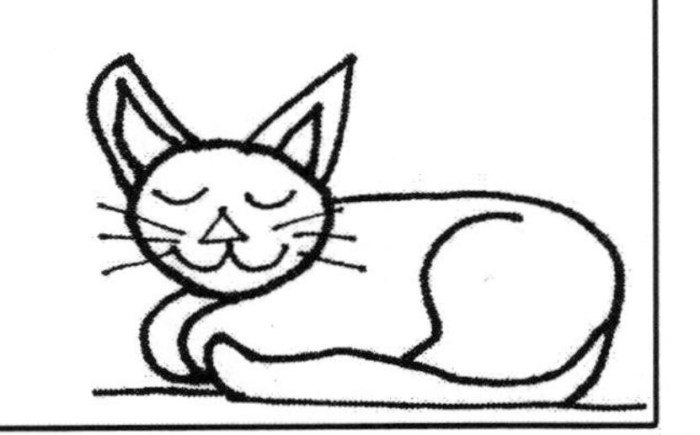

I have room in my heart
for all of me

Room in your heart

Every part of you deserves love.
Every strength, weakness
faith, fear
quirk, quality and misguided thought
has served
the perfect
ongoing
evolution of You.

Time to be
the person
of my
dreams

The self of your dreams

Stop trying to be someone you're not.
Any idea of who you think you're supposed to be
isn't half as amazing
as who you already are.
Stop trying, motivating, or forcing yourself
into some other shape.
Expand into what is natural for YOU.
THAT is the self of your dreams
and that
is far, far more extraordinary
than any person you think you "should" be.

Relax.
Breathe.
Let it
unfold.....
Ahhh.....

Relax

There is no pushing the river
or forcing the seed to grow.
There is a perfect order
that takes care of itself –
guiding the acorn into the oak.
There is no rushing
the vast, beautiful movement of the Universe
or the magnificent unfolding of You.

Ahhh.....

Autumn feeling

There is a time for letting go
and a time to let things fall away.
There is a time for clearing
and sorting
and reflecting
and for slowing down.

Later,
there will be a new harvest.

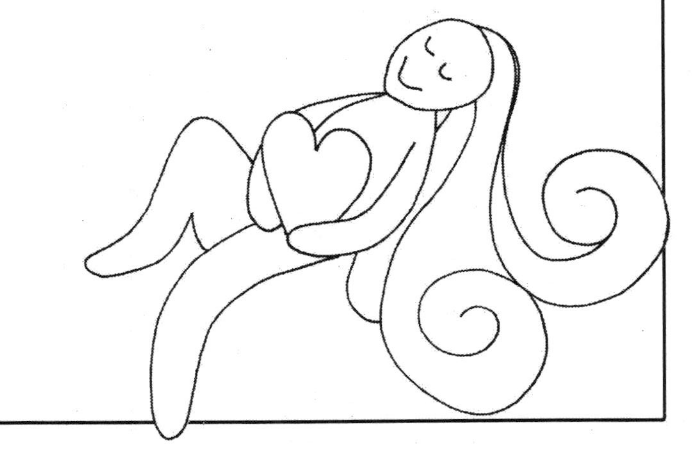

Feel
into it
CB

Feel into it

Take the time to take it inside.
Let your heart try it on
and stretch out into the possibility.
Some things fit.
Some things don't.
Make any alterations you need.

Come back
into
your body

Come back into your body

Your body is your friend.
Even when it hurts
or feels sad
it's trying to talk to you
about important stuff.
It's safe
to come out of your head
and listen to all those
feelings
gut intuitions
and sensations.
Life is richer and more beautiful
with all your inner and outer senses!
Be in your friendly body.
It's wise
ALIVE
and it loves you!

Yes
I
allow
now

Allowing now

It's how we relate to our nows that's important –
not that we control them.
The discomfort comes
from thinking any moment should be
different than it is
and that it should do what our mind says.
But every moment is part of the Big Picture
and every now is held in Bigger Hands.

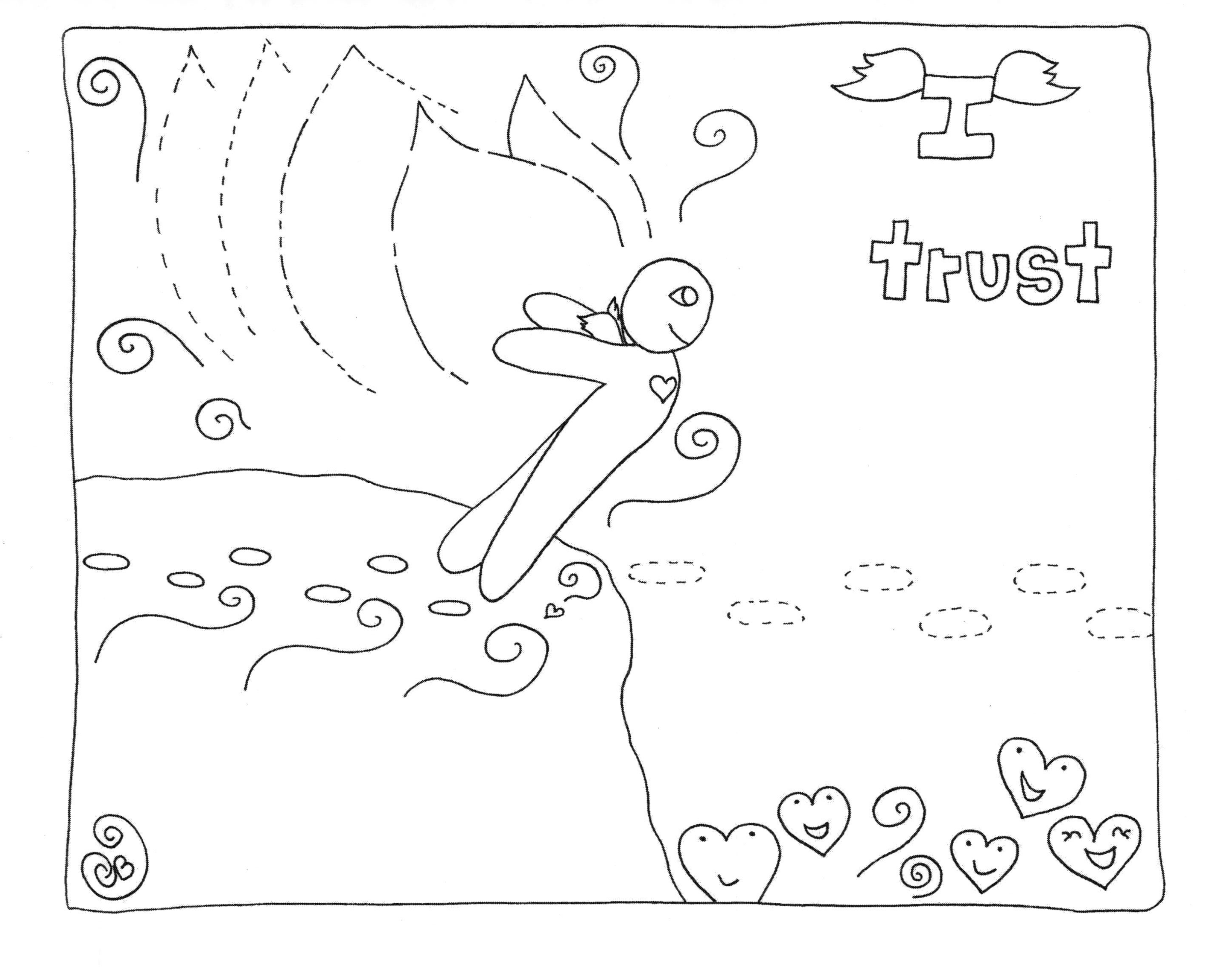
I
trust

Trust

Trust your heart
because it really does know.
Trust your body
because it really is your friend.
Trust life
because it really does love you.

EVERYTHING
is some form of
the Universe
loving
me

The loving Universe

You are standing
in a friendly Universe –
even when things don't SEEM to be working out.
No matter what it looks like
life is offering itself to you.
It serves you
guides you
and loves you
with everything it has.

Don't you just love that one?!
TOTALLY!
I am good
Awesome!
Fantastic!
Super!
Splendid!
Marvelous!

<u>You are good</u>

It's okay to stop striving
toward what you already are.
You are good.
You come from good.
You are goodness expressing itself!
Already.
Always.
Effortlessly.
It's only when we try to prove it
or earn it
that things get confusing.

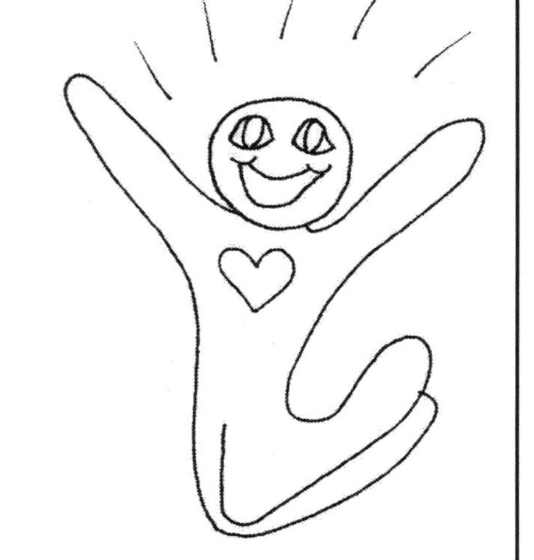

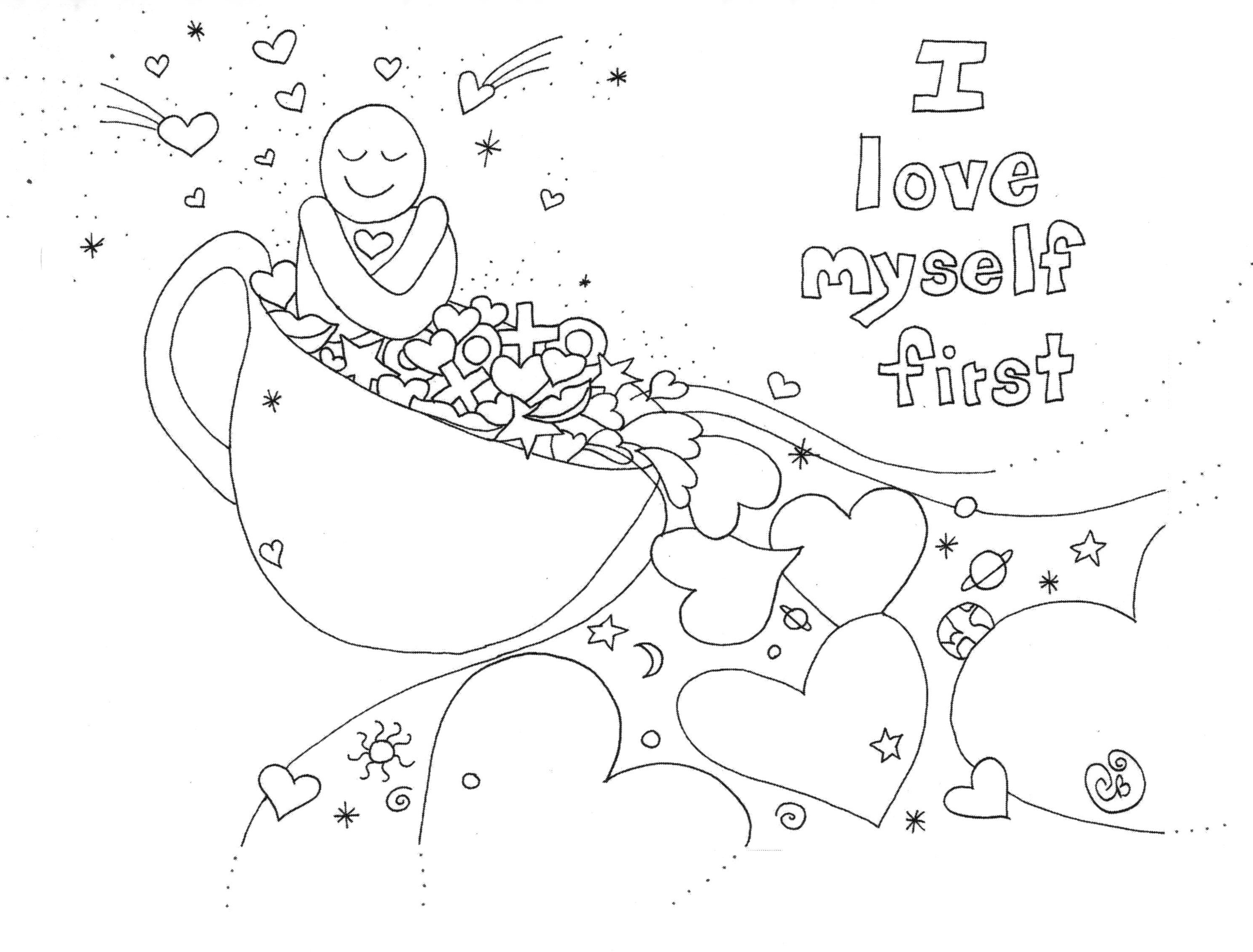
I love myself first

Self-love first

You are taking care of the Universe
when you take care
of the piece of the Universe called you.
That's your whole purpose –
to be you and adore you!
And it's the most powerful way
you could ever help anyone.
Create change in you, love you, uplift you
and you make change, love and joy
available for everyone!

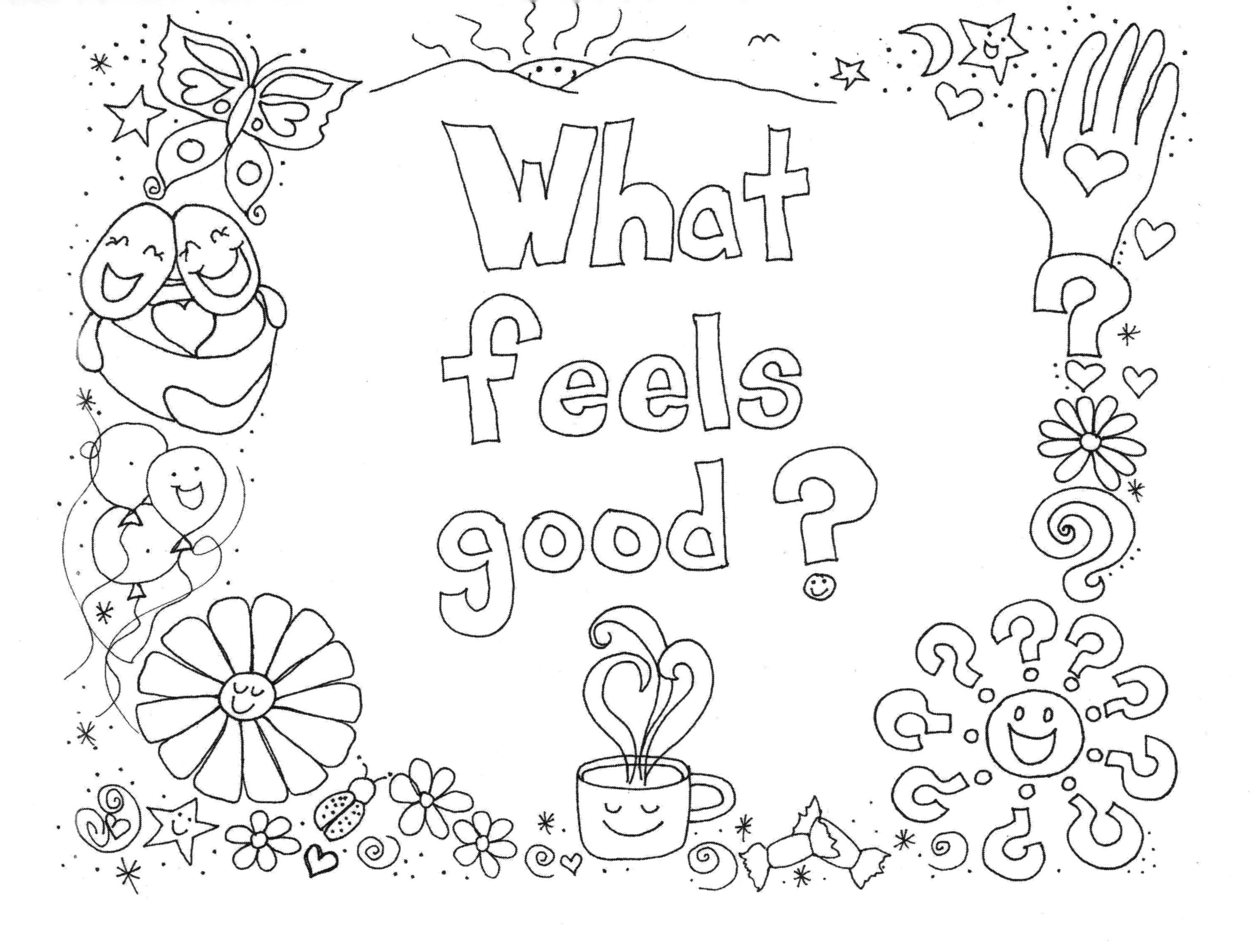
What feels good?

Pleasure matters

Pleasure matters

Make pleasure a priority.
Whatever YOU enjoy
is medicine that changes your entire experience!
Pleasure is good for your health.
It improves your mood
and de-stresses your mind
which benefits everything you do
blesses all your relationships
and honors your being.
Take the time.
It feels good.
It IS good.
And it matters.

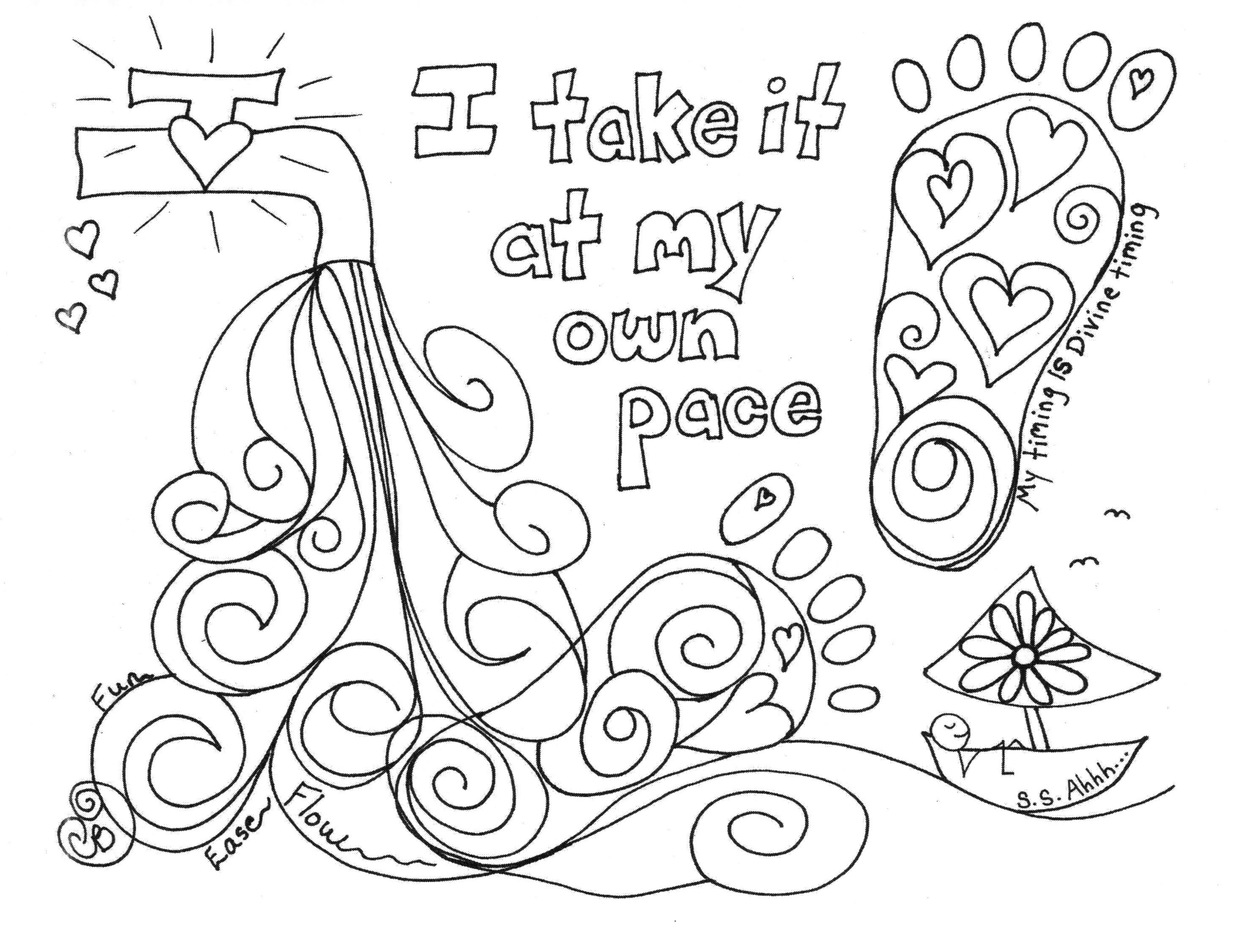
I take it at my own pace
My timing is Divine timing
S.S. Ahhh...
Fun
Ease
Flow

Your own perfect pace

There is no race
no contest
no prize for finishing first
or last.
When you do things
as you are ready
and in a way that feels good to you
there is an integrity
a solidness and rightness
rarely in need of going back to "redo."
You are moving as you were meant to
when you follow inner timing
and you are honoring your rhythm
within the perfect harmony of All Things.

Self-love affects everything

Self-love affects everything

You ARE the Universe.
What you do for you
you do for All Things.
Treat yourself with kindness and respect.
Have compassion for every part of you.
Believe in your goodness.
Support your own dreams.
Then you add more of all that
to the entire Universe.
Everything is connected.
Loving you
is your most direct way
to create more love everywhere.

Be kind
to your
past

Be kind to your past

Every version of yourself
was necessary.
Without them you wouldn't be who you are now!
Bless yourselves
and love them all –
especially the one you're living today.

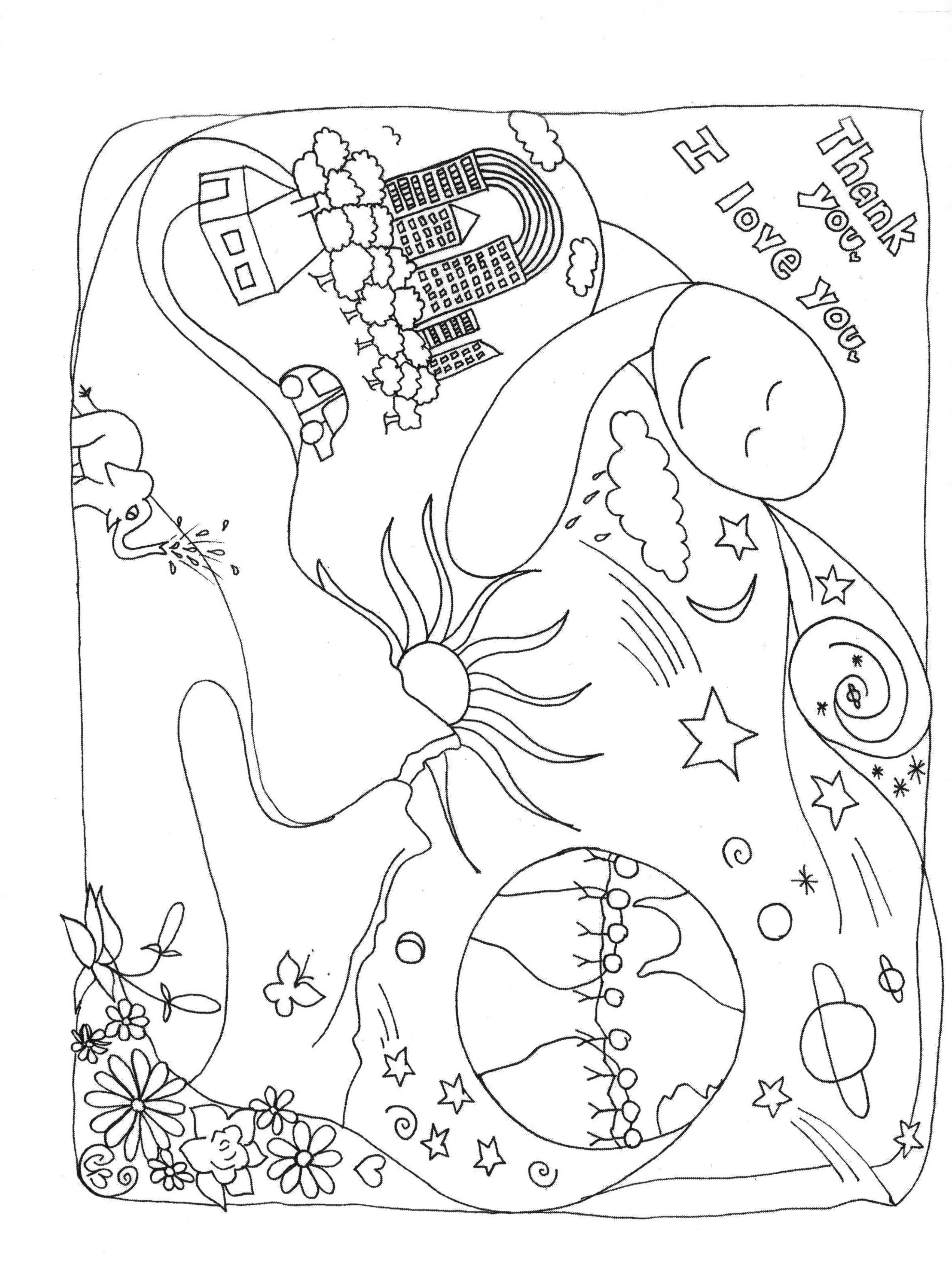
Thank you.
I love you.

Love and thanks

Gratitude.
Gratitude.
Gratitude.
There is so much to appreciate
about every day.
Love on purpose
and you gift yourself
with the whole world.

I am love ♥ I am love ♥ I am love ♥
I am love ♥ I am love ♥ I am love ♥

You are love

Surrender to your own goodness.
Rest easy and be carried
by the loving energy that animates everything –
including YOU.
It's your nature to love
and to express love inward and outward
because you ARE love
from your tiniest atom to your biggest hug!
Relax
into the effortless love of YOU.

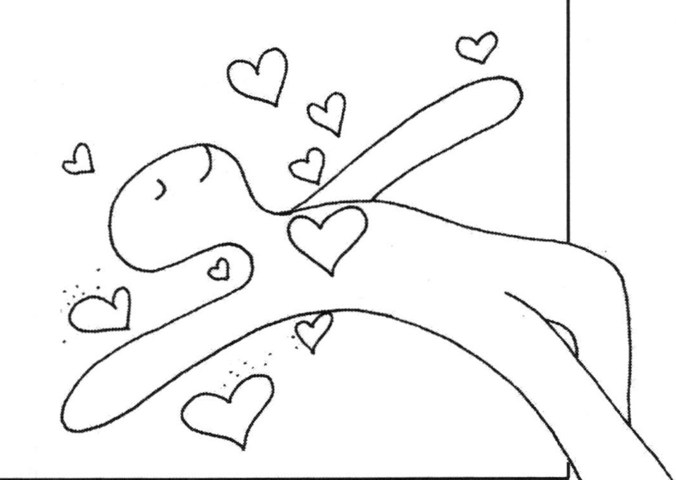

Find a kinder way to look at it
That's not how I thought it would go
The Universe really loves me!
a huge gift!
Good job! Excellent! That totally works in my favor!
but I bet this way will be even better!
I can see how this is
I'm so proud of me!
Wow! Look at all the beauty here!
Doing great!

A kinder way

Being mean to yourself
is never a good idea.
Faultfinding and harsh criticism
jam up your system.
They short-circuit
your thinking, your body, and all communication.
There are almost no options
when you look at things with that state of mind.
But look with kindness for what you love
and it brings a magic that will change your life!
All around you and in you
are things to admire.
Shine a light on those
and you create a beautiful, flowing world of possibilities.

I send love
and let go.

Let go and love

Stand in love
and let it go
knowing that it's all taken care of.
Things are always working in your favor
however it might appear.
Whatever it was or is
bless yourself
by turning it over
to all the Bigger Forces that adore you.
And bless yourself
by being the love that you are
right now.

Eeny, meeny, miney, LOVE!!
Let
self love
make the
decisions

A good decision

Let go of any fear about making the right choice.
Any decision made out of self-love
is a good one.
And it will work to everyone's benefit
because then –
no matter what action you take –
it's backed by kindness
self-encouragement
and integrity.
And no matter how many times you change directions
you'll keep walking a path that supports
the unique
worthy
naturally joyful life that you want!

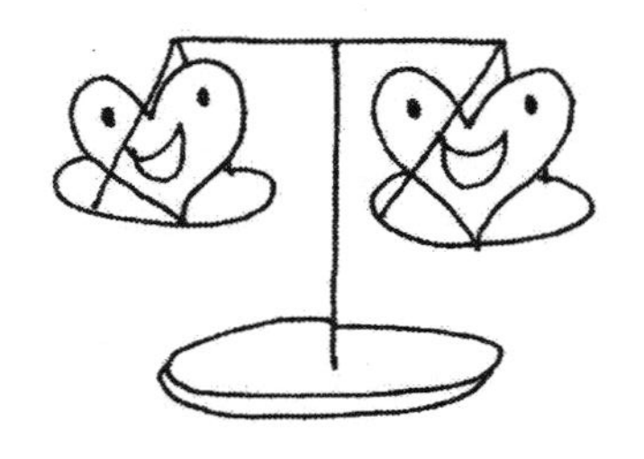

It's
safe to
change

It's safe to change

Let the world be bigger
than your past experience.
What worked then
may not work now –
and it's not what's keeping you safe.
LIFE is safe.
And your gorgeous transformation
is certain, supported, and unfolding perfectly.

My angels have me covered!

Angels

We're all in this together.
All the beautiful souls –
visible
and invisible –
cheering for each other!
Did you know that every step you take
is blessed and celebrated?
Go ahead –
it's safe to walk your path.
It's a parade route, you know!

Life is loving
??
MYSTERY
?
Even the unknown

Life is loving

The known quantity
is not the only quantity.
What you know now
used to be part of the Great Unknown.
Don't be afraid of the Mystery –
it loves you
and is planning your surprise parties!
Now's a great time to put your dancing shoes on!

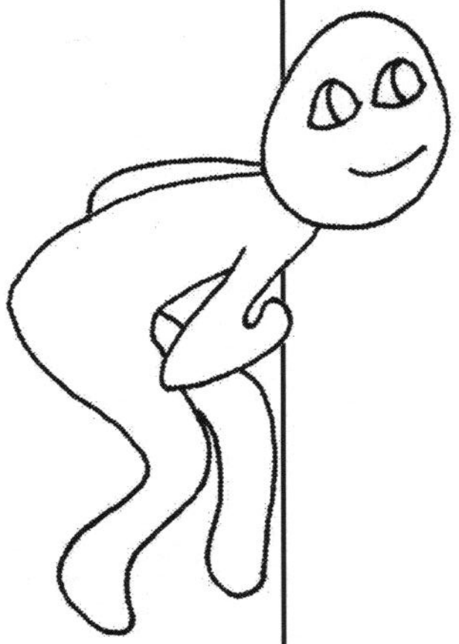

It's ok
to be
still and silent

Still and silent

Doing can be fun!
And mostly, it's optional.
Busyness, achieving, hustle and bustle
can sometimes just cover up
the song of YOU.
Just sitting there
breathing
you are a magnificent piece of music
that sings out into Existence
making everything more beautiful.
Be still
and listen
to the concert of your own, effortless being.

It's good to rest whenever I need to
Now

Rest

Needing to rest
doesn't mean there's something wrong
or that you're not "keeping up."
It means your body, mind and spirit
are busy doing important things.
Just because you can't see it
doesn't mean it's not valuable work.
Inactivity
(Inner activity)
has vastly more power
to help you heal, grow and transform
than any visible, outer "doing."
Enjoy your rest!

I am Partnership
I am balance

True partnership

Be with yourself.
Be a partner to you.
You have everything to offer you –
everything to share
everything to give and receive
everything is inside of you.
Yin, yang.
Left, right.
You are whole.
And
you are in partnership
with the entire Universe.
There is no way for you to be alone.
You are The Infinite Divine
in union
with Itself.

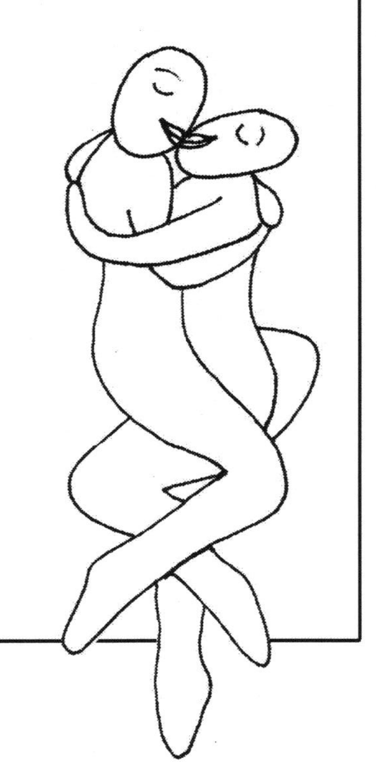

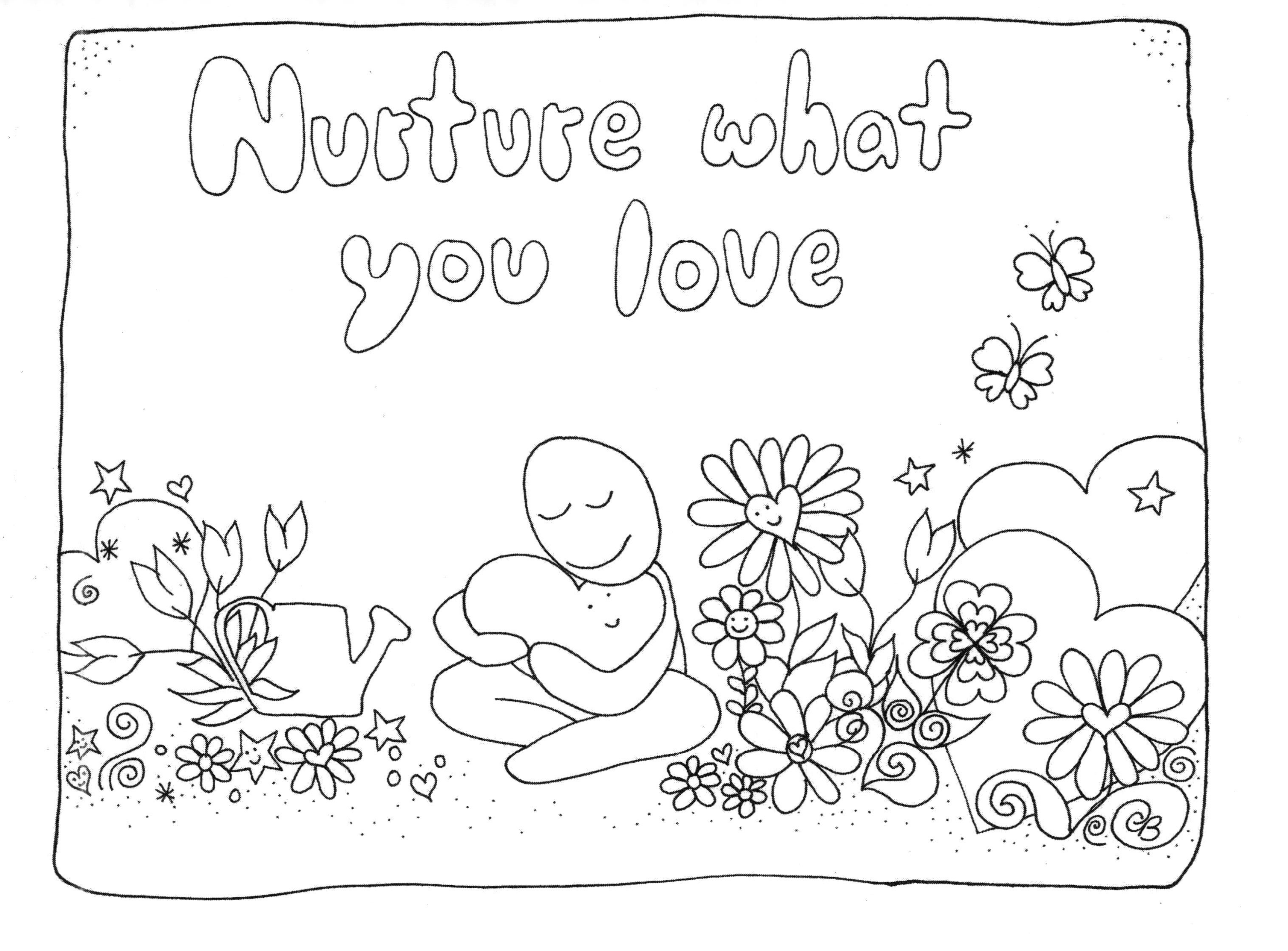
Nurture what
you love

<u>Nurture what you love</u>

You can choose
what you give your time and thoughts to.
You can decide
what's important to YOU
and what you'd like to see grow.
What you give your loving attention to
will thrive!
Do what you love!
Spend time with people and things
that light you up!
Don't live your life
by autopilot and obligation.
You have the simple power
to nurture a life you adore.

I am
Safe, held
and cared for.

<u>Held and cared for</u>

The Universe not only knows you're there
but it's caring for you all day long.
You are seen with Adoring Eyes.
There are Bigger Arms
joyfully holding you!
And you are guided by a Divine Heart
that loves you beyond measure!
There is a Bigger Picture
and you're a cherished part of it.

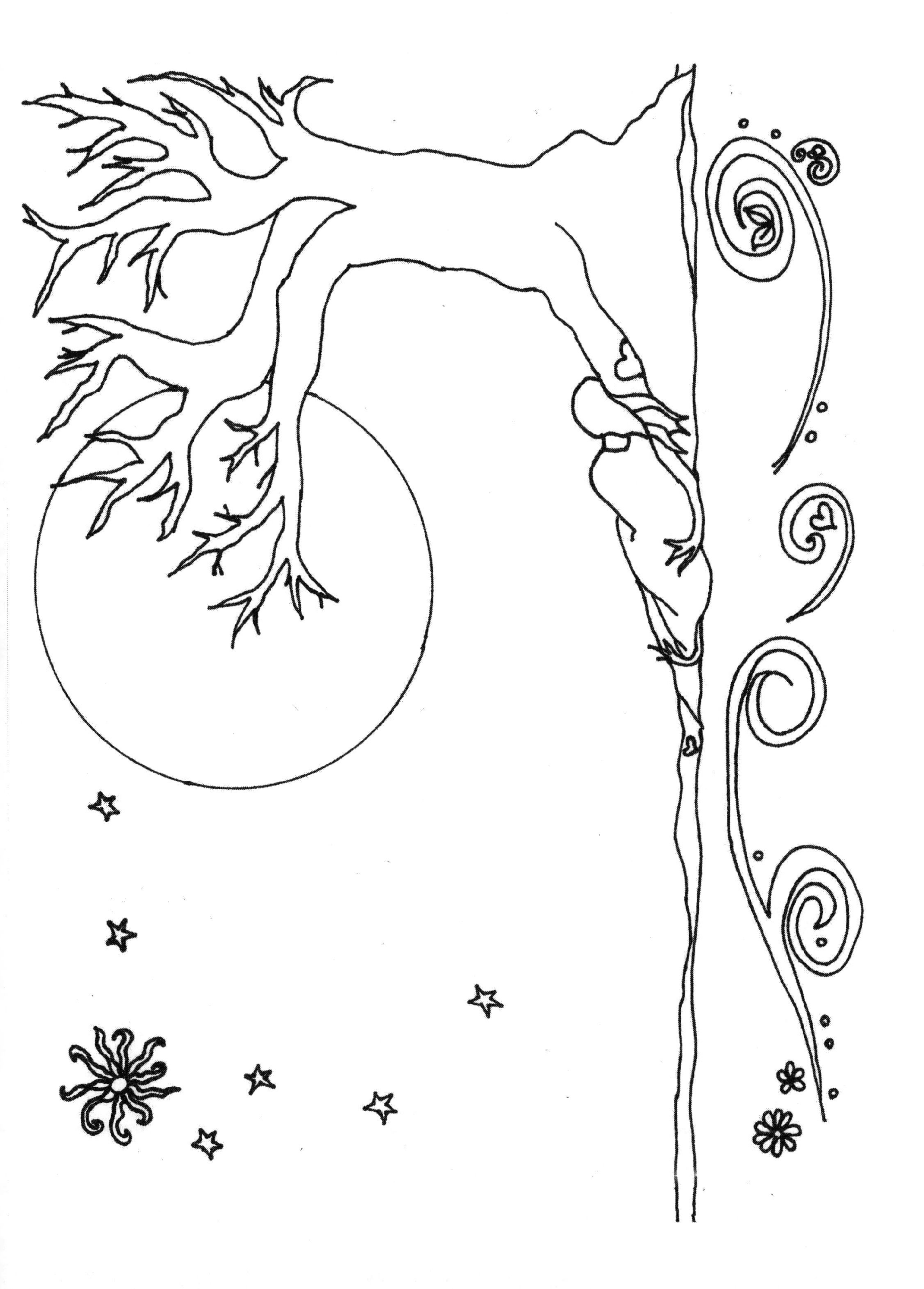

Winter feeling

Stillness is necessary
while deep
invisible movements
prepare for the spring.
Time to turn your vision inward
and let it drift
and rest
in the starry void
of infinite possibilities.

All is well

All is well

All the masters and sages have been saying it throughout time.
They know that ultimately we are safe.
That we can trust that everything is unfolding perfectly.
And that all is well.
(It really is.)

Please turn book
This way

And lastly...

My take-home message

All the pages in this book
are my take-home messages.
Take them home to your warm hearth.
Gather around the sweet fire
and read the stories to every part of you.
Wrap every part of you up
with reassuring blankets of light
and the truth
that the Universe adores you
and could not be more proud!
Rest.
Laugh!
Celebrate
with all of the angels
all of the stars and galaxies
and all of Existence!
They have been sending you messages
love letters
and songs that rejoice in your brilliance
for all the days of your life.
And they will all keep loving you
forever and ever more.

About the Author

Christina Brittain holds a Masters of Fine Arts in Dance, a Masters level professional diploma in Expressive Arts Therapy, and a wide variety of certifications in energetic medicine. Christina grew up naturally combining arts and energy for personal growth and awareness. One of her earliest memories was of being taken to see a Native American shaman. By age 5, she was drawing, writing poems and dancing to intentionally express her feelings and shift her mood. Today, her inspirational cartoons, intuitive counseling practice, and workshops focus on the conscious use of thought and imagination to create more inner freedom and joy. Christina is the Vice President of The Patrice M. Cox Foundation, which is dedicated to helping people learn how to love themselves. She is also the author of *The Lighten Your Vibe Coloring Book.* Christina lives in San Diego, surrounded by beauty and an extraordinarily wonderful group of friends. You can find out more about her work at www.ChristinaBrittain.com and www.PatriceMCoxFoundation.org.